D1275982

Isolation and Alliances

AN AMERICAN SPEAKS TO THE BRITISH

BOOKS BY WALTER LIPPMANN

A PREFACE TO POLITICS

DRIFT AND MASTERY

THE STAKES OF DIPLOMACY

THE POLITICAL SCENE

LIBERTY AND THE NEWS

PUBLIC OPINION

THE PHANTOM PUBLIC

MEN OF DESTINY

AMERICAN INQUISITORS

A PREFACE TO MORALS

INTERPRETATIONS 1931–1932

INTERPRETATIONS 1933–1935

THE METHOD OF FREEDOM

THE NEW IMPERATIVE

THE GOOD SOCIETY

U.S. FOREIGN POLICY: SHIELD OF THE REPUBLIC

U.S. WAR AIMS

THE COLD WAR, A STUDY IN U.S. FOREIGN POLICY

ISOLATION AND ALLIANCES: AN AMERICAN SPEAKS TO THE BRITISH

With William O. Scroggs

THE UNITED STATES IN WORLD AFFAIRS 1931

THE UNITED STATES IN WORLD AFFAIRS 1932

Isolation and Alliances

AN AMERICAN SPEAKS TO THE BRITISH

by

WALTER LIPPMANN

INTRODUCTION BY THE EARL SPENCER

An Atlantic Monthly Press Book

Little, Brown and Company · Boston

LIBRARY OF CONGRESS CATALOG CARD NO. 52–1196

FIRST EDITION

ATLANTIC–LITTLE, BROWN BOOKS
ARE PUBLISHED BY
LITTLE, BROWN AND COMPANY
IN ASSOCIATION WITH
THE ATLANTIC MONTHLY PRESS

PRINTED IN THE UNITED STATES OF AMERICA

Introduction

THE Sulgrave Manor Board were very lucky to secure Mr. Walter Lippmann to occupy the Watson Chair in the first lectures since 1940, and anyone who heard them must have been greatly impressed by their charm, lucidity and good sense.

All those he gave — whether at Oxford, Cambridge or in London — were crowded with enthusiastic and expectant audiences, among which were many undergraduates.

In fact, Mr. Lippmann's reputation and unique position had made his audiences expect something great — and no one can have been disappointed. Not only were the lectures great, but his replies to questioners were clear and masterly.

When so much ignorance is shown concerning Anglo-American relations, it was exceedingly refreshing to hear an American speaking with such understanding of our problems on this side of the Atlantic and to hear such wise and interesting ideas on current topics, especially in the year of the Presidential election.

Introduction

We are very grateful to Mr. Lippmann for these lectures, which we are glad to see printed in book form so that they reach a wider public in this country and abroad.

SPENCER
Chairman, The Sulgrave Manor Board
London, England

Contents

I

The Tradition to 1945

I THINK I should tell you that when I received Lord Spencer's letter saying that the Sulgrave Manor Board was inviting me to take the Watson Chair this year, I did not at first appreciate what it was going to mean to talk about the subject which he proposed. However, my wife and I agreed at once when we read the invitation that here was the best possible excuse for coming to England in the spring. Only after that did I realize that it might fairly be argued by any one of you that in undertaking to explain our foreign policy in terms of our public opinion I would be offering to explain one mystery in terms of another.

I began to consider the duties which went with the honor of this appointment – and to reflect upon the circumstance that there has been no Watson lecturer since my friend Sir Frederic Whyte spoke at Rhodes House in January 1940. After these tremendous years the Watson lecturer, if he is an American, would feel silly if he spent any time explaining to anyone in either country how vitally important Britain and America are to each other, and how necessary it is that we should understand one another. After the days we have lived through together I feel quite free to talk to you about my own country without apology, without advocacy, and without exhortation.

I began by wondering what thread to follow in the mighty maze and complication which these twelve years have brought into our affairs. Then, as I was turning the subject over in my mind, trying to sort out my ideas, Mr. Churchill arrived in Washington. Once again, and as always in the past, I felt better because he had come. I had been in Washington during all of his previous visits as Prime Minister. I had learned that they have, if I may say so, several aspects. There is, of course, the serious business at hand. But over and above that there is a public aspect, a kind of extra dividend, in a Churchill visit. All Americans enjoy it hugely – including those who look carefully to see, once he has departed, whether the Star-Spangled Banner is still waving over the White House. The feeling which everyone enjoys is not without historical and symbolical significance. I can describe the public aspect best by saying that it is as if somehow or other Westminster Abbey and the Tower of London had arrived, and several times a day with many horns blowing were proceeding majestically and exuberantly up and down Constitution Avenue.

But in this visit, besides the substance and besides

the monumental and symbolic features, there was something else, something unusual which bears directly upon these lectures. I became aware of it myself while I was listening to Mr. Churchill's speech to the joint session of the two houses of Congress. I had heard his two previous speeches, and I have heard many other addresses to Congress by the heads of governments and by the heads of states. This was unlike any of the others. It was unlike, I venture to think, any speech that has ever been delivered before in a representative assembly.

I hope I shall not offend the purists of the British Constitution. The Prime Minister – so it seemed to me – talked to the American Congress in the mood and posture of a responsible Minister determined to win a vote of confidence from a reluctant House. It was apparent, I thought, that the Prime Minister knew that he had only a slender working majority in the Congress of the United States – something like eighteen votes if nobody came down with the flu. It seemed plain enough too, I thought, that in order to gain support on both sides of the House he had decided that he must appease a part of the Opposition, even though that meant much pain to some of us among his own back-benchers.

The fascinating novelty of the occasion sprang of course from the fact that the Prime Minister would soon have to deal with the same subject in the other Parliament. Here, then, we were witnessing for the first time a demonstration of what the structure of the British-American connection has come to be in the course of these twelve years. It was all the more significant because it could not have been contrived deliberately.

Here was the proof that our affairs have become so enormously intricate and so deeply enmeshed that the business of conducting our relations has overflowed all the conventional channels of diplomacy. What we have grown into is a working connection which no one – not the most far-seeing – anticipated clearly. We who are involved in it do not as yet begin to understand well enough. There are no treaties or statutes which define the whole connection. There are no recognized terms, so far as I know, in the political sciences which we can use to describe our relationship.

There is contact, confrontation, controversy and collaboration at all the levels of the two governments. Our relations are no longer that of Foreign Office with State Department. Virtually all the great departments of the two governments are in direct communication with one another, and not only that – within each of the departments and bureaucracies of the two governments there is all manner of direct dealing

— of planners with planners, and of administrators with administrators and of technicians with technicians.

We have now learned — and Mr. Churchill's speech in Congress made it evident — that the developing contact would have to go beyond the executive departments of the two governments. The connection having become so complicated, Parliament and the Congress were sure to be carried along and to become involved with each other. We have been brought to a point where the Prime Minister found he had to obtain the support both of the Congress and of Parliament on the same controversial issues of foreign policy.

Where this will carry us we do not know. But the two governments, though they are separate and sovereign, are learning that each must shape and conduct its policies in response not only to its own representative assembly but to the other representative assembly as well. And since representative assemblies are elected by voters, those who deal in international affairs are now accountable to two constituencies, and they have to acquire a practical working knowledge of public opinion not only in their own country but in the other.

With these preliminaries you will expect me to furnish a clue or two as to how to go about understanding and treating and dealing with American public opinion.

This calls for something more than reliable information about what happens to be the prevailing opinions on particular topics – for more than the kind of information which can be had by using the modern devices for sampling opinions. That something more is, of course, to be able to interpret reports of contemporary expressions of opinion. To do this, a working knowledge of the traditional forms in which Americans habitually think and feel about foreign affairs is, I am sure you will agree, indispensable if one is to judge the meaning and weight of opinions.

Now American history is brief. It is, I know, tiresome to hear this said again. But we are indeed a young nation. And in remarkable degree, the main ideas with which we approach foreign affairs are still those of provincial America. They are the ideas which became habitual during the century and a half before the American nation became a Great Power. The traditional and fundamental themes of American foreign policy are now known as isolationism. That is a term, however, which must be handled with the greatest care, or it can do nothing but confuse and mislead.

It began to be used about 1900 after the Spanish-American War, but it was not widely used until

1914 – until the great debates about American intervention in the two world wars and about American participation in affairs outside the Western Hemisphere. The word isolation is highly charged with emotion – with the acute anxiety which twice in this century, so many, on both sides of the ocean, have suffered, as, facing defeat and disaster, they waited for American intervention, waited until it was almost too late – waited perhaps until it was too late to make a good peace. I have shared these anxieties. Yet, speaking as an old hand in these debates, I should like to point out to you that the term isolation is misleading as the name of any significant contemporary American movement in foreign affairs.

During the hard-fought battles over intervention the isolationists were the party of neutrality and of pacifism. They prevailed in the sense that the American nation refused to enter either world war until we ourselves were attacked and were, therefore, compelled to go to war. This has caused many abroad and at home to think of the United States as trying – rather foolishly and in vain – to be a kind of big and boisterous Switzerland, a sort of pushing and untidy Sweden – until, at long last, by dint of great argument and exhortation the Americans were aroused, though they are always in danger of relapsing, to do their duty as befits their power in the great world.

According to this legend, the American colonists along the Atlantic seaboard achieved their independence because of the follies of King George III and his Ministers. They found themselves with a vast, an empty and an enormously rich continent at their backs. The legend has it that as they moved into this vacant paradise, they forgot their European heritage. They became wholly immersed in their internal affairs, chiefly in making money. Thanks to the Pax Britannica, they were so secure that they did not need to bother themselves with the affairs of the Old World. In the enjoyment of their too many blessings, which they never seem to weary of boasting about, they became soft and timid – until they were stung into action first by the Kaiser and Admiral von Tirpitz, and then by Hitler and the Japanese.

This is, of course, a false picture and many Europeans are now beginning to appreciate that fact when they discover, often to their dismay, that if it was hard to arouse the sleeping giant, it is also hard to quiet him down again. The term isolationists, and the mythology which has grown up around it, suggest passivity and lethargy. The word isolationist conceals the dynamic and expansionist energy of the American nation. It suggests that the United States did not have a foreign policy until recently. All that is quite untrue. The United States has never been neutral in the European sense. It has always had a very active foreign policy, of which the central purpose has been the determination to expand across the continent from the Atlantic seaboard to the Pacific Ocean.

American foreign policy has been in this sense continuous from the middle of the eighteenth century and throughout the nineteenth century. It has been a policy designed to open up the continental territory, to consolidate that territory firmly within the American union, and to make that territory and the approaches to it invulnerably secure as against all other powers. To accomplish these ends the American people have used diplomacy and war.

The struggle to acquire and consolidate what is now the national territory of the United States lasted until the close of the nineteenth century. It began with the French wars of the eighteenth century. The American colonists participated in these wars, always for American reasons. Officially, so to speak, the struggle for the national territory ended in 1890, when the last of our thirty-seven wars with the Indians was concluded.

Those whom we now call isolationists are the true believers in the foreign policy of the men who conquered and settled the American continental domain.

The memory of their struggles against foreign powers, and against the Indians and against the wilderness, has been the living tradition of the Americans who have played leading parts in this century.

Isolationism, then, is not pacifism and withdrawal. It is a deposit of ideas from the experience of conquering, consolidating and securing the national homeland. The traditional American attitude towards European powers, towards alliances with foreign nations, towards war and towards peace, can be understood only when the words of American statesmen – of Washington, Jefferson, Monroe, Wilson, Roosevelt and Truman – are read in the historical context of this struggle for the continent.

American foreign policy has not been so much a reflection of the old colonial cities on the Atlantic seaboard as it has been the instrument of the pioneers and settlers who pushed their way across the Appalachian Mountains into the Mississippi Valley, across the Rocky Mountains and on to the Pacific coast. They did not find that this territory was a vacant paradise. They had to open it up. They had to clear the wilderness. They had by diplomacy and war to work their way past the Great Powers – past Great Britain, France and Spain. They fought the Indians, who in the early days had often been armed against them by the Great Powers. They fought the

Mexicans, who were the heirs of Spain in North America.

The famous phrases and injunctions and precepts which are the currency of the American tradition were minted in this struggle.

Consider, for example, Washington's injunction in the Farewell Address, which he published in 1796, when he had decided not to be a candidate for a third term. "The great rule of conduct for us in regard to foreign nations," he said, "is in extending our commercial relations to have with them as little political connection as possible." For, he went on to say, "Europe has a set of primary interests which to us have none or a very remote relation."

When Washington laid down this rule that we must have as little connection as possible with Europe, he had just completed the ratification of Jay's Treaty with the British Government. This treaty was being attacked bitterly on the ground that the United States was being forced to ransom its own property, the northwest posts, by humiliating concessions in commerce, shipping and maritime rights. But Washington and his Cabinet insisted on ratification because the treaty meant that the last frontier post occupied by British soldiers on American soil would be evacuated and the Ohio Valley opened up to settlement. When Washington spoke of political separation from Europe, he was deeply conscious of being surrounded — of being contained — by great unfriendly foreign powers.

Let me say a few words about another of the texts. It is from the address which Thomas Jefferson delivered at his first inauguration in 1801. The famous words are "peace, commerce, and honest friendship with all nations, entangling alliances with none." Shortly after this disavowal of entangling alliances Jefferson performed the diplomatic feat of buying the Louisiana territory from Napoleon Bonaparte. He seized a golden opportunity which was presented to him because France and Great Britain were at war. Jefferson, having no entangling alliance, did in fact negotiate with both powers, and he used his neutral position to make a bargain which brought into the union the Mississippi and Missouri valleys.

Isolationism, I repeat, is the deposit of this fundamental American foreign policy. The principle of the policy was to keep a free hand in order to expand westward to the continental limits. In any current European usage of the words American isolationism is not neutralist or pacifist. By nature and by mood it is not prudent and it is not retiring. The isolationists of the twentieth century have wished to isolate not merely the American continental domain and the Western Hemisphere. In the last analysis they have wanted to isolate American decisions and actions, to have the final word wherever Americans are involved. They carry with them the thought and feeling which has come down from those who in the eighteenth and nineteenth centuries managed in one way or another, by war and by diplomacy, to expel all the foreign powers who blocked the westward expansion of the American people.

Many other influences have reinforced this basic pattern. Americans have always had a moral conviction that they were conquering a continent not as an empire to be exploited but as Jefferson, or perhaps it was Madison, put it, to be a new domicile of freedom. Americans have never thought of their territorial expansion as imperial conquest. They have always believed that they were opening the territory to all mankind – by which they meant all of the European mankind from which they were themselves descended. It was the European governments which they hoped to see expelled from the New World. The governments, they believed, were political tyrannies. The European social order, moreover, did not recognize that all men are equal. The Americans were mastering a wilderness which was inhabited by savages, and they were opening it up to all men who wished to escape from class, from privilege, from bigotry, and from persecution.

But the new nation formed out of families emigrating from all the countries of Europe was bound to know a certain tension. The ancestral lands in Europe are not altogether foreign. The separation is not complete. In times when feeling runs high, Americans are drawn back to, and then they push themselves away from, the old fatherlands. Whenever the United States has been the ally of one European power and the enemy of another the assimilation of Europeans into the American nationality has been interrupted. This morbid experience is known in America as hyphenization.

The traditional foreign policy – that of regarding the American system as separate from Europe – of keeping Americanism unentangled with loyalties in Europe, is adapted to this inner problem.

What I have been saying about the general character of American foreign policy is also, I think, a useful introduction to the differences between the two political parties in foreign affairs.

The Democratic Party is descended directly from the party which was in office when by diplomacy and by war the United States acquired the Middle West and the Far West. Throughout American history it has been the party of bold designs. The Democrats made the Louisiana Purchase. They declared the Monroe Doctrine. They annexed Texas. They conquered the Southwest and California. The Democrats were in office during both world wars. They proposed the League of Nations and helped organize the United Nations. All the famous declarations of American purpose and policy – from Wilson's Fourteen Points to the Truman Doctrine – have been made by Democratic Presidents.

On the other hand, the Republican Party has played the leading part in realizing, in making actual, the fundamental American purpose. The Republicans presided over the settlement and over the development of the West. Under Lincoln they won the Civil War and consolidated American territory in one union. The Republican Party has been dominant in, one might almost say in possession of, the territory which for a century and a half it was the paramount object of American foreign policy to acquire and to absorb.

That goes a long way to explain why the Republicans of the Mississippi Valley are so deeply disposed to what the world knows as isolationism. The Repubcan Party was in power continuously throughout the second half of the nineteenth century and until the First World War. It was in power even, as the saying goes, when now and then it was not actually in office. Moreover, the impulse which had carried the American nation across the continent did not stop when the pioneers reached the Pacific coast. The Republicans were in power when this happened, when the frontiers within the continent disappeared. They pushed the American frontiers still farther outward towards the west. They bought Alaska. They annexed Hawaii. They conquered the Philippines.

In the light of that it is not too difficult to understand why the Republicans tend to be isolationists when they look across the Atlantic Ocean back towards Europe, and why they tend to be imperialists when they look across the Pacific at Asia.

Around about the turn of the century the central purpose of the traditional American foreign policy had been achieved. In the eyes of all but a small adventurous and romantic minority our western expansion was completed: in the conquest of the Philippines we had in fact been carried beyond our natural and proper limits.

The Philippines were much too far away to be thought of as destined to become American territory. More than that, a permanent occupation of the Philippines would have violated the basic assumption, the inner moral sanction of the American expansion. Americans had always regarded it as self-evident that any territory they acquired would be organized into states and would be admitted into the Union, and that the inhabitants – who would be predominantly of European stock – would then be assimilated into equal American citizenship.

Americans have never wanted to rule over any territory which could not be admitted as a state into the Union or to govern peoples who could not be assimilated. The Philippines, obviously, could not be admitted into the Union and their people could not be assimilated into the American nation. In American eyes, therefore, they were beyond the natural and the moral limits of American interest and American destiny, and in conquering them from Spain our western expansion had, so to speak, overshot its mark.

The fulfillment of the historic purpose of American policy coincided with the radical change in the world balance of power. The necessary condition under which the United States had been able to expand to the Pacific Ocean and to consolidate its continental territory had been the European equilibrium under the Pax Britannica. The architects of our foreign policy – Washington, Jefferson, the two Adamses, Madison, Monroe – had known quite well that it was the preservation of the balance of power in the Old World which made it possible for the weak nations of the New World to isolate themselves, while they were developing, from interference by the Great Powers of Europe. This had, however, been forgotten by the later generations.

The German challenge of 1914 put in doubt what no American then alive had supposed could ever be put in doubt. It challenged the existing order which was deemed to be natural and not historical. No one in America had anticipated this, and few were prepared to understand it. The nation had always faced towards the west. Now it had to turn around and to recognize that there was a great threat from the rear, where all had so long been so secure. Instead of continuing to look forward towards the west, where there had always been the American promised lands, the nation had to look backward across the ocean to the countries from which it had come.

Ever since then we have been learning by hard experience that the old order of the world is broken, and that it cannot be restored, and that the making of a new order is a task which our generation may hope to see begun but cannot hope to see completed.

The task of Americans who have had a part in events since 1914 has been to adjust, transform and convert traditional American ideas to the new necessities. That has been, that is proving to be, a most difficult thing to do.

Within the lives of one generation we have been called upon to remake our fundamental conceptions of the nature of the political world. By conscious reasoning, by imagination rather than long experience, we are having to transform our deepest habits and our oldest traditions. I do not think I have misled you in dwelling so much upon the American tradition. The great revision of the tradition, which history demands of us now, has to be made against the well-nigh instinctive feeling ingrained by the experience of a century and a half, that our expansion, our union as a single nation, and the security which we have enjoyed, were achieved *despite* the powers of Europe – were achieved, to use the contemporary words for these things, not by co-operation but by unilateralism and by insisting upon a free hand.

There lies the explanation of the Wilsonian ideology – the first great American effort to meet the New World situation. The principles which President Wilson enunciated when we were drawn – so reluctantly and with such deep misgivings – into a war on the continent of Europe were the improvisation of a man who knew he was forced by events to take a course which he, like all the older Americans, thought we had forever renounced. The Wilsonian doctrine was the adaptation of the American tradition to an unexpected necessity – that of returning to Europe, of fighting on the soil of Europe, and of reuniting politically with European nations.

President Wilson had hoped that he could avoid it, but he was finally driven to accept the necessity of following a policy of intervention in Europe. He was himself, however, an American fundamentalist, a sincere and deeply convinced believer in the postulates of the traditional policy. Only the extreme provocation of the unlimited submarine war, combined with the dire peril of the West in 1917, brought him to take the epoch-making decision to raise an army by conscription and to send it across the Atlantic Ocean.

The Wilsonian ideology was President Wilson's attempt to reconcile these new and heretical imperatives with the old, with his own deeply personal American orthodoxy. The Wilsonian thesis was, if I may put it in this way, that, since the world was no longer safe for the American democracy, the American people were called upon to conduct a crusade to make the world safe for the American democracy. In order to do this the principles of the American democracy would have to be made universal throughout the world. The Wilsonian ideology is American fundamentalism made into a universal doctrine.

The Wilsonian system of ideas does not recognize that America is one nation among many other nations with whom it must deal as rivals, as allies, as partners. The Wilsonian vision is of a world in which there are no lasting rivalries, where there are no deep conflicts of interest, where no compromises of principle have to be made, where there are no separate spheres of influence, and no alliances. In this world there will be no wars except universal war against criminal governments who rebel against the universal order. The Wilsonian ideology is a crusading doctrine, generating great popular fervor from the feeling that war is an intolerable criminal interference with the nature of things. The necessity of going to war is an outrage upon our privacy and upon our rights.

Therefore, all wars are wars to end wars, all wars are crusades which can be concluded only when all the peoples have submitted to the only true political religion. There will be peace only when all the peoples hold and observe the same self-evident principles.

In the Wilsonian ideology an aggression is an armed rebellion against the universal and eternal principles of the world society. No war can end rightly, therefore, except by the unconditional surrender of the aggressor nation and by the overthrow and transformation of its political regime.

The Wilsonian ideology has, it is fair to say, dominated American political thinking and has shaped American policy ever since it was formulated. As late as 1943, for example, Secretary Hull, who was a personal disciple of Wilson, and a lifelong true believer, came home from the Moscow Conference and announced that "as the provisions of the four-nation declaration were carried into effect there will no longer be need for spheres of influence, for alliances, for balance of power, or any other of the special arrangements by which, in the unhappy past, the nations strove to safeguard their security or to promote their interests."

One can hardly exaggerate the compelling, and until very recently, the all-pervading acceptance of this ideology. The explanation of its enormous influence is, as I have been arguing, that in its motives, its modes and its manners, the Wilsonian ideology is a twentieth-century variant of the historic American fundamentalism.

In all the debates, beginning in 1914, and in the debates which are still in progress – for example over the appropriations for foreign aid in the present Congress – the Wilsonian ideology has shaped the arguments of those who have favored intervention, participation in the League of Nations and the United Nations, the Truman Doctrine, the Marshall Plan, the North Atlantic Treaty, the intervention in Korea, the Mutual Security Act.

One can argue, in fact it is often argued at home, that this extraordinary series of measures could never have won popular support unless the highly charged emotions of the Wilsonian ideology had been aroused to support them. The American people and the Congress, it is argued, would have refused and resisted these measures had they not been backed by the proclamation of crusades against the Germans, the Japanese, the Soviets, the Chinese Communists, and Communism in general – had the American people not been fired by promises that these crusades would end in a universal order where all peoples, including the objects of the current crusade, would swear allegiance to the same purposes and would observe the same principles.

There is no denying that this has been the easiest and the quickest way to force through Congress measures which call for the use of American troops and the appropriation of American money for grants abroad. But this method of dealing with our people has, as many are now coming to see, established no political and moral foundation for a settled and steadfast policy. The great Utopian promises have too often turned out to be dust and ashes, and they no longer arouse the fervor and the ardent hopes of 1918 and of 1945.

The measures, it is becoming evident to many, which are promoted by resorting to the ideological incitement, by applying the technique of the crusade, tend to become gravely, and sometimes irreparably, deformed in the very process of getting them enacted. The original ends and intentions of these measures have been almost invariably noble and necessary. But the means employed to carry Congress and the people to accept those ends have often aggravated the troubles which the measures were meant to alleviate.

In my view it is becoming increasingly plain that the Wilsonian ideology is an impossible foundation for the foreign policy of a nation, placed as we are and carrying the burden of our responsibilities. Our people are coming to realize that in this century one crusade has led to another. After the first crusade we were not able to prevent the next war that was coming. We were not prepared for the war when we had to fight it. And twice we have not known how to settle the war when we had won it. Twice in one generation we have gone around this deadly cycle.

Voices are beginning to be heard, asking whether we can break the deadly cycle, and by taking thought and by mastering ourselves resist the destructive impulses of our democracy – which is to be too pacifist in time of peace and too bellicose in time of war. In this deadly cycle of pacifism and bellicosity we, and perhaps the other democracies as well, have wanted disarmament, neutrality, isolation, and if necessary appeasement. Then, as the wars which we did not avert, which we entered reluctantly and unready, rose to their climax of violence and victory, we have felt that our righteous wrath could do with nothing less than unconditional surrender, total victory, the total reform and regeneration of the vanquished – all of them the necessary conditions of the everlasting peace in which we could again disarm ourselves and could again relapse into a private and self-regarding existence.

There is, I need hardly tell you, no ready-made and well-tested philosophy and doctrine of international society which we can confidently and easily turn to. I do not suppose you have such a doctrine and philosophy either, or we should have heard something about it from you. But perhaps together, by genuine frankness in our discourse with one another, we may be able to fashion out of the old wisdom of mankind and a fresh appreciation of the new realities a philosophy which can guide our policy.

We have much to do. For we have now entered into a time when the Wilsonian ideology is fading away, while none that is as yet cogent and persuasive has come forward to take its place.

In my second lecture I shall try to have something to say about more recent developments.

II
Facing a New World Situation

IN MY FIRST lecture I discussed the traditional American foreign policy and I tried to show how it has persisted in this century in the form of the Wilsonian ideology. Today I shall be discussing the situation in which we now find ourselves. I shall begin by saying that looking back on the past from the place where we are now laboring, it is important to note that the critical period in American thinking about foreign affairs began only very recently.

It began, I would say, as we have learned to recognize that in the making of war and peace we are no longer, as we had been in our early history, minor participants or, as we were throughout the First World War and well into the Second, an auxiliary power, a supporting and reinforcing power, called in to redress the balance of the Old World. Our first realization that we were a primary power came, I imagine, during the Pacific War against Japan. This war was predominantly an American responsibility. It was the first important war we have ever fought against a Great Power in which we were ourselves the principals. But that was in the Pacific. It was not until after that, not until about 1947, that we began to think of ourselves as having a primary interest and responsibility – not only in the Pacific but in Europe as well.

I would mark the change in our attitude towards Europe as beginning with Mr. Bevin's call upon us to intervene in Greece. It was only then that the American people, and indeed American officials themselves, began to realize how radically our position in the world had altered.

The radical novelty of our present position is, as seen with American eyes, that we have now become a principal power. In the first German war the role of the United States had been to reinforce the allies. President Wilson, Admiral Sims and General Pershing contributed much to the result of the war. But they did not conduct the war. The supreme commander on land was Marshal Foch. At sea the war was directed by the British Admiralty. In diplomacy, though President Wilson addressed the masses of the people, he did not speak for the governments. In the First World War we did not regard ourselves as one of the allied powers, but only as an associated power.

For some years before 1939, many Americans, including President Roosevelt, knew that a war was coming and that America would almost certainly be involved in it. But even the most far-sighted thought that America would participate in the second war, as it had in the first, in order, as the saying went, "to aid the allies." In 1939, in 1940, even in 1941, none, I think, foresaw that before the war was concluded, the supreme commanders in Europe and in Asia would be Americans and that the combined chiefs of staff would sit in Washington.

But now it appears to be taken for granted almost everywhere that though we consult with our allies, the final decisions in the grand strategy of the great conflict are made in Washington. Even as late as 1946, when Mr. Churchill made his address at Fulton, Missouri, almost no one foresaw – I do not know of anyone in America who foresaw it – how near we were to the day when the United States would undertake to be the principal power in the organization of a world-wide coalition.

The issues and problems of our foreign policy are, therefore, quite novel and recent. One must keep that in mind in reading the speeches in Congress and in the present political campaign. Much of the language of many of the phrases may be old and trite. But we are not, in fact, arguing the old questions of 1914, 1917, and of 1939, 1941 – shall we, or shall we not, intervene in Europe?

If our problems *now* were what they were in 1914 and in 1939, we and the rest of our friends could be at ease. The Americans would be a nation which had resolved its doubts and had agreed on its tasks and its duties. When the second war ended, our people were for all practical purposes unanimous in the conviction that never again would they hesitate before aligning themselves with the nations that resisted aggression, that never again would they withdraw from the organized international effort to prevent war.

But since 1945 we have been discovering that the postulates of the old controversy, and of the decisions by which we resolved that old controversy, are profoundly altered. We have been learning that the question is not whether we shall go to the support of a coalition of powers aligned against aggression, that it is not whether we are willing to collaborate with an international organization. Our relations with our allies have, we are seeing, been transformed. Our problem has become, so it appears to us, not whether we will join the allies, but whether the allies will stay joined with us.

For this new and unexpected role our experience has not prepared us and our traditional philosophy is not a guide. The Wilsonian ideology – we can now see – is a way of thinking which served us as long as our role in the world was that of an auxiliary power only, as long as our responsibility was not primary and original, and as long as the interests at stake were not immediately and directly American interests.

In our role of auxiliary the Wilsonian ideology served to justify intervention in Europe to our own people. It allowed us the luxury of standing apart from our principal allies, particularly from Great Britain and France, which had direct interests and commitments all over the world. Standing apart, we could support them and we could refuse to support them, we could approve and we could criticize what they did. We could measure all claims on our support, particularly in the colonial and dependent areas of Asia and of the Middle East, by our own ideological standards. All that was possible when we had only to fit ourselves into a coalition which already existed, when we did not have to organize a coalition which did not exist.

The recognition of this new role is very recent and it is by no means as yet general. So recent is it that we find ourselves playing today a role which we did not expect to play when the Senate ratified our membership in the United Nations, when Congress voted the Marshall Plan, even when the Senate first ratified the North Atlantic Security Pact. All of these great international measures – the UN, the ECA and NATO – were conceived and developed on the postulate that America was still aiding the allies. They have been transformed since they were enacted – as the radical change in our role became impressed upon us – and they have been remodeled hastily and crudely into instruments for leading and organizing the coalition.

It would be a miracle if, in two or three years, we had improvised the policies, the programs and the skilled administration for the task which is not only radically new in American experience, but is in so many respects without precedent in the experience of any other nation.

It has often been said, I know, that America must play the part in the twentieth century which Great Britain played so brilliantly well in the nineteenth century. An American is bound to be very much aware that in one respect the analogy is imperfect. He is bound to wonder whether the United States can re-enact the role of Great Britain when there is no nation which can re-enact the role of the United States. More than a century ago Canning said that he had called in the New World to redress the balance of the Old, and in 1917 the prophecy was fulfilled when Great Britain and France were able to draw upon the reserves of the United States.

But no nation can now play the part that we have played. There is no large, rich and powerful nation with the same vital interests as our own and sharing our ideals, which could redress the balance in our favor if we became engaged in a war which we lack the power to finish. For us there can be no Wilson and no Roosevelt across the ocean. We have to shape our policies with the knowledge that there are no strategic reserves upon which we could draw if our plans miscarried.

This may help to account for that element of anxiety and tension which pervades so much American thinking these days about foreign affairs.

When we turn from explaining and interpreting, as I shall now do, and put ourselves in the position of making up our minds about what lies ahead, we move into the realm of speculation and argument. It is the essence of the matter that our policies are not formed but are in the process of being formed. All I can do here is to describe in broad outline the course which I believe we can best take. I am not, of course, predicting that we shall take it. I do venture to think that it would find acceptance among our people if it were fully considered and were well developed by men on both sides of the Atlantic.

We were on the right course, as I see it, during the war – specifically, between 1942 and 1945, in the period between Mr. Churchill's visit to Washington immediately after Pearl Harbor and the death of Roosevelt and the defeat of Churchill in 1945. During those years we had a close partnership, one might call it an organic alliance, which managed the business of war and peace in the Western world – managed it for what we have come to call the Atlantic Community.

The Atlantic Community had its combined staffs, its combined boards, its unified commands, and perhaps most important of all its agreed diplomatic actions. The Atlantic Community had a foreign policy. It was affiliated with the Soviet Union for the purposes of the war. For want of a better word, I use the word affiliation. The relation was certainly not a partnership. It was not really an alliance. It was a kind of cobelligerency among rival and not friendly Great Powers, who, until they had been attacked by the same enemy, had just about managed to coexist.

The Atlantic Community was affiliated also with China, not much more intimately or candidly than with the Soviet Union.

These kinds and degrees of partnership, alliance and affiliation were not invented a priori. They grew out of the realities of our position and the necessities of the struggle. Our great mistake, I would say, is that we did not found postwar policies upon these realities and necessities. They represented the true structure and relationship of power and interest in the world that we are living in. They showed that structure, not as it might have been designed in theory, but as experience was showing that structure to be.

Had we done that, had we made the wartime structure of relations the foundation of the postwar system, had we made it plain before the war had ended that we were resolved that the Atlantic partnership was to continue and was to endure, then it would have been as the Atlantic Community, rather than as separate states, that we could have entered the postwar negotiations to make the peace treaties and to establish the United Nations.

Why we did not do this is a long and complicated story, and much of it is still obscure. But what I have been saying was proposed and pressed upon our governments. There were men on both sides of the ocean who argued that the Atlantic Community should be consolidated prior to a settlement with the Soviet Union about the future of Germany, prior even to the organization of the United Nations.

The proposals were rejected. They were held to be a departure from, they were held to be in conflict with, the Wilsonian principles of a universal society.

Mr. Hull was then the Secretary of State, and Mr. Hull was a disciple of President Wilson, more orthodoxly Wilsonian than President Wilson himself had ever been. Moreover, Mr. Hull had played no important role in the partnership by which the war had been conducted. Yet he was President Roosevelt's main, and in fact his indispensable, liaison with the Congress of the United States in all matters that dealt with postwar policy.

In Mr. Hull's mind, the mere notion of maintaining the Atlantic Community after the war was over, and of entering the United Nations as a community, was a vicious heresy — a violation of the Wilsonian commandment against alliances, against spheres of influence, and against the balance of power.

Having said this, I should not leave you to think that I think we have a monopoly of the mistakes that have been made. I am a visiting lecturer remembering his company manners. But perhaps I may say that I do not recall hearing any serious argument from this side of the Atlantic against the course we were both taking together. In any event, we took the course which dissolved the partnership that had been tested in the war. We agreed, with conviction on our side of the Atlantic certainly, to identify the international order with the existence of a universal society, composed, as we conceived it then, of theoretically equal and entirely separate national states.

We plumped for what was, as I was saying yesterday, the internationalism of the isolationists. In their conception of the world, when it is pure and ardent, when they have not been pushed into compromises with the hard substance of things, there are no legitimate entities between national states on the one hand and the universal society on the other, between the atom and the cosmos. The whole drift and impulse of their doctrine, moreover, is to make more and more national states out of the larger existing political units, to propagate new states by fission, and thus to populate the universal society with an ever-increasing number of feeble governments.

That this plunge into unmitigated universalism was the wrong course to take in 1945 became clear in 1947 and 1948 when, finding it necessary to set up the Marshall Plan and the North Atlantic Security Pact, we turned back to the Atlantic Community. In doing that we were admitting that the postwar policy of 1945 had been a painful and a costly detour, and that we must now work our way back to the right road. But, of course, we are finding it harder to repair the error now. For now we are having to recreate our Western partnership in defiance of, in the very teeth of, the Soviet Union. Had we never dissolved the Atlantic system, Stalin would have found himself dealing with us after the war as he had had to deal with us during the war.

I do not say that he would have liked it, but at least

he would have been rather more used to it, and certainly he would have had to respect it — to respect it at least as much as he respects it now that it has been revived in NATO.

In any event, after the detour into universalism, we are now back on the main road, and I think I may say that increasingly our interests in the Atlantic Community are tending to be the deciding consideration of our foreign policy. That at least can be said of official thinking and planning in the State Department and in the Pentagon. In Congress and among the people the traditional modes, though they are receding, are still dominant. Practical politicians do not as yet like to speak of foreign affairs except in the universalist language. It was on their advice that the concrete measures which were required for our intervention in Greece and for aid to Turkey were blown up into the universalist terms of the Truman Doctrine and the policy of containment.

The Korean war has brought an impressive demonstration of how the Atlantic Community has now become paramount in American military policy. In the controversy last spring between General MacArthur and the chiefs of state, the deciding reason for limiting the war to the Korean peninsula, for not expanding it into China, was that American strategic air power is not only committed to the defense of the

Atlantic Community but that it cannot as a matter of technical procedure be employed except with the full and willing collaboration of Great Britain and France.

Until the great controversy over General MacArthur, it was supposed by Congress, by the general public, by most soldiers, including of course General MacArthur himself, indeed even by most airmen, that, because we had a stockpile of atomic bombs and the planes to carry them, strategic air power was a uniquely American weapon which could be governed by American decisions.

The MacArthur controversy forced many who had taken all this for granted to study the situation closely and to listen – for the first time – to the serious and sober officials who had not hitherto been much in the limelight. It did not take them very long to prove conclusively that without the bases and facilities of our partners in Western Europe the strategic air force would be like a high-powered automobile in a jungle country where there are no roads.

I think it would be correct to say that General MacArthur's challenge brought to the surface, and established clearly for the first time, the fact that the military relationships between America and the European members of the Atlantic Community are mutual, that American military power depends upon its alliances and that we are in fact, in hard military fact, members of a community.

The realization that American military power is not self-contained and autonomous has had a profound effect on the American attitude towards our alliances in Western Europe. It has knocked the foundation out from under those who, like General MacArthur, have in effect been arguing that our interests in Europe are at best an expensive form of philanthropy and that our true destiny is to go it alone in the Pacific and in Eastern Asia.

We have by no means heard the last of this argument, or of the very active people who make the argument. But since the hard military facts were disclosed authoritatively, the influence of the isolationists in American military circles has been declining rapidly. This new knowledge is exercising a spreading influence in Congress and in the press. It has come to be understood, to put it in the broadest popular terms, that the soundest military doctrine is represented by Eisenhower rather than by MacArthur. Unless all the signs fail, the coming election will confirm the fact that the Atlantic alliance is now the cornerstone of our foreign policy.

But in saying that it is now the cornerstone, I would not wish you to think I am saying that our foreign policy is already consistently constructed upon it.

It is not. That is in fact the great business we have in hand. We are now engaged in constructing the foreign policy which is suitable to the alliance – in working out the positions and the programs, that is to say, which the alliance can best support and promote, which will best preserve and support the alliance. I need hardly say that these labors are a task for the allies. If I speak of the American part of them, it is because that is what I have been brought here to do.

The North Atlantic Security Pact is a military alliance which, when it was formed in 1948, was addressed to the particular fact that the Red Army stands inside Europe on a line which runs through Germany and Austria, and that it was then capable of overrunning Western Germany, the Low Countries and France, without meeting effective resistance.

When the treaty was first brought forward, it was the accepted view in American military circles that the reason why Western Europe, though defenseless, had not already been overrun was that the Soviet Government was deterred by the knowledge that this would mean a general war in which the United States strategic air force would come immediately into action, and that after that the whole military potential of the United States would be brought to bear.

The Security Pact was presented to the Senate, and by all of us who worked for it and supported it, as containing no more than the formal registration of a situation which already actually existed – namely, that Western Europe had no defenses of its own against invasion, that American military forces in being and potential provided the defense, and that if a war of aggression was started we would surely be involved. What the treaty did, we said, was to make all these facts, which no one disputed, into a formal guarantee. The *de facto* would become *de jure*. The Soviet Government would then be on notice, as the Kaiser and Hitler had not been, that a war of aggression in Europe would mean war with the United States. This guarantee would, we said, give a sense of security to the people who live in the path of the threatened invasion.

This was the original American conception of the alliance. Under criticism and pressure from France it had soon to be supplemented. Remembering the long delays in the two world wars before the United States intervened, the French demanded some more convincing proof of American intentions than the words of a treaty. Our response to that was to give a pledge that we would maintain a few divisions of American troops in Germany during the life of the treaty. Then no one – no Russian, no Frenchman, no German – could doubt that we would be involved in the war from the first day of hostilities.

We used, at the time, to describe these American

divisions as the plate-glass window in the jewelry shop. They were, we recognized, not nearly strong enough to protect the jewels. But if the robbers had to break the window, they would make so much noise that the whole neighborhood would be aroused.

When the formal guarantee had been reinforced with a token force of American divisions, a third phase in the evolution of the alliance began. It began with the demand that Western Europe be made capable of repelling an invasion in case the threat of atomic bombardment and of the full mobilization of American military power should happen not to be an adequate deterrent.

The deterrent power of the American Air Force and of its atomic bombs was said to be a declining asset. For the Soviet Government itself had solved the problem of making atomic weapons, and, moreover, the Soviet defenses against bombardment were growing stronger. There is, in fact, an influential school of American military thinking which holds the opinion that the aerial defense is forging ahead of the offense.

Nevertheless, the demand for an army to defend Western Europe against the Red Army was not well received at first in American military circles. The root of the American objection to the idea was that we do not like what the proposal obviously carries with it – namely, that in time of peace we shall maintain a large standing army. We think of ourselves as an island, as a continental island to be sure, but nevertheless as an island surrounded by the oceans of sea and air. We raise ground armies only during our wars, and we raise them as auxiliaries, as expeditionary forces serving with our sea and our air power, and we like to disband our armies when the war is over.

It was not easy to persuade the American military leaders to accept the idea that it is necessary or possible to organize the defenses of Europe on the ground. The pressure to do this came from our allies in Europe and from American civilians.

In the months just preceding the North Korean aggression in June of 1950, the conversion of the Pentagon had, however, made considerable progress. That summer, finding ourselves actually fighting on the ground across the Pacific Ocean, the idea of creating an army in continental Europe on the other side of the other ocean became a main object of American military policy.

About August of 1950, the Pentagon and the State Department agreed on the raising and equipping of an army in Western Europe that would be capable of fighting a successful defensive battle with as much of the Red Army as was then, or could soon be, deployed in Europe.

This decision was based on the assumption that what had happened in Korea could be taken as a rehearsal in miniature of what would probably happen in Europe. The Communist armies would overrun the poorly equipped non-Communist armies. We must not repeat, therefore, the mistake we had made in Korea, where we had failed to establish a strong South Korean army and had failed to keep American troops there to guarantee American assistance.

This was such a big and such a new decision that it required the approval of Congress and renewed support from the people. For most of the army we then had was already engaged in Korea and there were no troops to spare for Western Europe. Because of the fighting in Korea the decision to raise a very much larger American army was, however, acceptable to the country.

It was nonetheless unpalatable. The notion of sending a very large part of this newly conscripted army to Europe ran squarely into the question: why do not the West Europeans, who are twice as numerous as we are, provide at least the infantry for the defense of their own countries?

This led to a great deal of arithmetic in the Pentagon about how the number of divisions could be raised which the military planners then said were necessary. After counting up all the continental divisions that could be expected, and all the British, Canadians and Americans that could be spared, the planners found that they were still short by about twenty divisions.

It was at that point that the Administration plumped for immediate German rearmament. If it was true that Western Europe would soon be invaded as South Korea was then being invaded, if it took x number of divisions to defend Western Europe, if only x minus twenty were in sight within the NATO alliance, then there had to be German rearmament. What is more, there had to be German rearmament immediately.

The history of this momentous decision shows that it was taken for military reasons. It was the product of a military calculation starting from the postulate that there must exist in Western Europe an army powerful enough to repel the Red Army in Western Europe.

But, as we know, this military decision has brought us to matters which could not be settled by the military planners. It has brought us to questions which transcend military planning, to the questions of the place of Germany in Europe and in the world. These questions were bound to be raised soon enough. But our decision to rearm a part of Germany and to incorporate that part of Germany in our military alliance precipitated the whole German problem.

Facing a New World Situation

The great issue of policy which now confronts us is how we propose to solve the problem of the partition of Germany and of Europe. It will not do for us to follow a line of policy which implies, or which might seem to imply or could be regarded as implying, that our measures for the defense of Western Europe depend upon a continuing partition of Germany. We are in the gravest danger of finding ourselves in a wholly untenable position – that of making our military and political plans contingent upon the perpetuation of a divided Germany, and upon a German Government which can maintain itself only if Germany remains divided.

The measure of how much we have come to lean on the division of Germany is that we have allowed the Soviet Government to monopolize the idea of German reunification. We are not able to make our declarations about German unity convincing – because we have not been able to work out a European policy which leads under some known conditions to the evacuation of Germany. This is the hard core of the problem. It is that Germany cannot be reunited, the Iron Curtain cannot be rolled up, unless the Soviet Army withdraws. The withdrawal of the Soviet Army from Germany is inconceivable except as a result of a general agreement to withdraw all foreign troops. Yet the withdrawal of the British, French and American forces from Western Germany would compel us to make a radical revision of the strategic dispositions of the Atlantic Community.

We are becoming involved in what may become a grave predicament – that the strategic interests of the Atlantic Community, as we now conceive them and as we are now developing them, will come into direct collision, not only with the purposes of our great adversary – the Soviet Union – but also with the national interests of the German people.

No good can come of that, and surely we must realize that the military system of our alliance cannot be maintained, and that it will rest on quicksand, if in a country like Germany we cannot support the irreducible minimum national interests of the German people. We are unable to do that so long as our military interests are founded on the partition of Germany.

We have no choice, in my view, but to grasp the nettle by making the eventual evacuation of Germany by the non-German forces a plain goal of our own policy. I hope no one will think that I mean that we should, or that we could, agree to an unconditional or an immediate evacuation of Germany. I do mean that we must prepare ourselves to make a firm commitment to evacuate when the conditions are fulfilled which we judge to be necessary, which we have declared and have justified and have proposed for negotiation.

What are the necessary conditions? The Soviet Government in its note of March 10 laid down two conditions. The first was that united Germany should not join the Atlantic alliance. The second was that united Germany should recognize as permanent the provisional eastern frontiers marked out at Potsdam.

Quite evidently we cannot agree to withdraw our forces from Germany on these conditions. We cannot agree to a reunited and a rearmed Germany which has achieved not only sovereign equality but enjoys in addition an entirely free hand in its foreign relations. The Soviet proposal would enable Germany to manipulate the balance of power between the East and West, to maneuver against France and against Poland, and to dominate Europe.

The Soviet Government may think that a united armed and unbound Germany would have everything to gain by renewing the old alliance with Russia. But whatever the Soviet calculation, we cannot evacuate Germany if Germany has not become bound by her own sovereign choice and action within a European system.

What does that phrase mean, if we examine it in its hard concreteness? It must mean, I would say, first of all, a reconciliation between united Germany and France, a reconciliation which is so thorough that it can be sealed by a Franco-German alliance within which Germany and France would be bound to concert their foreign policy in Europe. Until France and Germany are fully at peace the forces of the Atlantic Community must keep watch on the Rhine. For a European system can exist only if at the heart of it there is a Franco-German partnership. Without that partnership, Europe cannot be united. With that partnership, a preponderance of the interest and weight of the European continent will be on the side of a European system.

The other Soviet condition is that united Germany should ratify the eastern frontiers of Potsdam. We cannot, I would argue, agree to that. To agree to it would be to leave the German nation with a national grievance which we had washed our hands of but which the Soviet Union could then redress. This would mean that we had renounced all our rights to participate in the settlement of Europe east of the Elbe, indeed east of the Rhine. For the settlement of these territorial questions will determine the relations of Germany with Russia and with Eastern Europe and in fact with the Eurasian continent.

My view is that we should make it a condition of the evacuation that united Germany, already allied with France, shall then negotiate a settlement with Poland which fixes their common frontier, contains also an agreement for the relief of the expellees, and an economic treaty.

If and when – but only if and when – there is a Franco-German-Polish understanding, can one speak with any seriousness about the unity of Europe or, as I should prefer to call it, a European system.

I do not mean to argue that the conditions which I have indicated are not very difficult to meet. They are very difficult. At best it would take a long time to meet them. They are not, however, impossible conditions. They are a sound position on which to stand while we work for a European settlement. No one can argue successfully that they are not the minimum necessary conditions of a secure and peaceable European continent. No one can argue that they violate the national interests of any European nation. The conditions are based on the principle, which is I think indisputable, that the unity of Germany and the unity of Europe are inseparable. As the champions of that principle the Atlantic Community would, I believe, win respect by deserving it.

It is, I am sure, of the greatest importance that the sincerity of our policy should not be in doubt. Now at best it would take a long time before the conditions of evacuation could be met. An all-German government must be formed and it must then prove itself by negotiating successfully with its neighbors. Only then would the evacuation take place.

The Soviet conditions, as they are now presented, would seem to offer a much quicker peace treaty and a much earlier evacuation. We must depend upon the intrinsic merits of the conditions to justify a prolongation of the occupation, which is what this policy means and requires.

But we can, and I think we should, give incontestable proofs that our conditions are serious, and that they are not devices for nullifying the commitment to restore the unity of Germany by the withdrawal of all foreign troops. We can do this best by proposing certain measures which would be taken as soon as our conditions are accepted in principle – when a constituent assembly to write an all-German constitution has been elected and a provisional all-German government has been formed.

The armies of occupation would remain until the new united German government had met the conditions which are necessary to the formation of the European system. But though these armies of occupation would remain in Germany, they might begin to withdraw by stages to the periphery, releasing Berlin and a large central region.

That would mark the end of the postwar situation in which the armies of the West and of the East stand face to face in the heart of Europe, and are crazily entangled with one another in Berlin. It would mark the beginning of a separation of the contending forces. It might lead – conceivably – to an armistice in the cold war.